CONTENTS

Any words appearing in the text in bold, **like this**, are explained in the glossary.

A POST-WAR WORLD

In 1945, the Second World War ended. It had been a **total war**. This means it involved nearly every country in the world. For the first time more ordinary civilians had died than soldiers. There had been terrible acts of racial hatred during the war and when it was over people all over the world had to deal with this.

The war had destroyed whole cities and millions of homes all over the world. Many countries had lost much of their wealth and the UK was nearly **bankrupt**. Food was in short supply, especially in the **USSR**. Only in the United States did people's incomes rise and the **economy** grow stronger as a result of the war.

Germany and Japan had lost the war and they were no longer leading world powers. The United States and the USSR were now the new world leaders. They had been **allies** during the war, but this friendship quickly ended. Their leaders had different ideas about how best to organize society. This developed into a new kind of war, the **Cold War**, where both countries developed huge stores of nuclear weapons but never actually used them.

The UK was no longer a superpower. Like other countries with **empires**, the end of the war brought demands for independence from **colonies** in Asia and Africa. African Americans in the United States demanded full civil rights.

A US Navy officer greets his wife and daughters on the dock at California, United States, after returning from duty in the Pacific.

From Television to the Berlin Wall

Pat Levy

www.raintreepublishers.co.uk
Visit our website to find out more information about **Raintree** books.

To order:
Phone 44 (0) 1865 888113
Send a fax to 44 (0) 1865 314091
Visit the Raintree Bookshop at **www.raintreepublishers.co.uk** to browse our catalogue and order online.

First published in Great Britain by Raintree, Halley Court, Jordan Hill, Oxford, OX2 8EJ, part of Harcourt Education.
Raintree is a registered trademark of Harcourt Education Ltd.

Editorial: Melanie Copland, Tameika Martin, and Lucy Beevor
Design: Michelle Lisseter and Bridge Creatives Services Ltd
Picture Research: Mica Brancic and Ginny Stroud-Lewis
Production: Duncan Gilbert

Originated by Chroma Graphics (Overseas) Pte. Ltd
Printed and bound in China by South China Printing Company

10 digit ISBN 1 844 43953 4 (hardback)
13 digit ISBN 978 1 844 43953 9 (hardback)
10 09 08 07 06
10 9 8 7 6 5 4 3 2 1
10 digit ISBN 1 844 43963 1 (paperback)
13 digit ISBN 978 1 844 43963 8 (paperback)
10 09 08 07 06
10 9 8 7 6 5 4 3 2 1

British Library Cataloguing in Publication Data
Levy, Patricia
From Television to the Berlin Wall. – (Modern Eras Uncovered)
909.8'25
A full catalogue record for this book is available from the British Library.

Acknowledgements
Corbis p. **22**; Corbis/Bettmann pp. **4**, **5**, **7**, **17**, **20**, **26**, **27**, **34**, **35**, **38**, **44**, **49** (top), **55**; Corbis/Hulton Deutsch Collection pp. **24**, **37**; Corbis/Pablo Corral Vega p. **39**; Corbis/Roger Ressmeyer p. **41**; Corbis/Terry Cryer p. **45**; Getty Images/Hulton Archive pp. **11**, **12**, **13**, **21**, **23**, **25**, **32**, **33**, **36**, **42**, **43**, **47**; Getty Images/Time Life Pictures pp. **6**, **31**, **46**, **49** (bottom); The Advertising Archive Ltd pp. **10**, **14**, **15**, **40**; The Bridgeman Art Library/Private Collection p. **30**; The Novosti Press Agency pp. **28**, **29**

Cover photographs (top and bottom) reproduced with permission of Corbis.

Every effort has been made to contact copyright holders of any material reproduced in this book. Any omissions will be rectified in subsequent printings if notice is given to the publishers.

The paper used to print this book comes from sustainable resources.

The hard times of war began to ease by the late 1950s and people felt confident about the future. New technologies were improving the quality of life and young people enjoyed wealth that their parents had never known as teenagers.

The technology of television signalled a new world, but the building of the **Berlin Wall** in 1961 was a product of the Cold War. People growing up in this period had good reason to feel hopeful, but they also had reason to be fearful.

American women enjoy the new products of the 1950s as they shop in Gimbels department store, New York, United States.

Tears and laughter

A woman, travelling to meet her soldier husband, remembers hearing news of the end of the war in a railway station:

"An old lady beside me burst out crying. I did the same, a soldier whom I did not know picked me up and swung me around, the spare engine standing in the station just sounded its horn for a full five minutes, everyone spoke to everyone else, we were all so happy."

(FROM *HOW WE LIVED THEN* BY NORMAN LONGMAN)

THE AFTERMATH OF WAR

Over a quarter of a million soldiers returned to their families in the UK from all around the world. Many UK cities were in ruins, people were still homeless, and food was still **rationed**. Women had worked during the war, but most were now expected to go back to being housewives. They were no longer the head of the household. The divorce rate rose by 50 per cent after the war as couples struggled to adapt to their new circumstances. In 1948, the National Health Service was set up in the UK, providing free medical care for everyone.

Picking up the pieces

Around the world people began trying to get their lives back to normal. There were about 40 million homeless people in China as a result of the war against Japanese occupation. Food was in short supply everywhere and in some countries people were starving. In the United States, over 120,000 Japanese-Americans had been forced to move into **detention camps** when the war began. These camps were poorly built, fenced barracks guarded by armed soldiers. When the prisoners were released from the camps at the end of the war, many found they had lost their homes and possessions because they could not afford to make their payments inside the camps. In Japan itself, people faced the effects of two **atom bombs** dropped on the cities of Hiroshima and Nagasaki.

Japanese-Americans line up for their meals at Heart Mountain detention camp, Wyoming, United States in 1942.

"We don't want you here!"

Victor Breitburg was a Jew who survived the **Holocaust** and returned to his home in Poland after the war:

"I saw a man who was still wearing the stripes [striped prison clothes] from the concentration camp. As I tried to approach him, two Polish people started to question him. 'Hey Jew, where are you going?...We don't want you here!' I was dumbfounded...I felt like shouting at them: 'You didn't help us; you turned us in; you are worse than the Germans.'"

(FROM NEVER AGAIN BY MARTIN GILBERT)

Deportations

In the USSR, people who the government thought had not supported them during the war were forced to go to labour camps, called **gulags**. Also forced into these camps were whole communities that were not trusted because they belonged to **ethnic minorities**. In all, about 15–30 million **Soviet** citizens died in the gulags.

Across Europe there were millions of **refugees**. In Germany alone there were 9 million refugees, called **displaced persons** (DPs). Some were people who the Nazis had **deported** from their home countries to work as slave labour in Germany. Others were citizens of countries in Eastern Europe. They had fled into Germany when Soviet soldiers began invading from the east towards the end of the war. Others were Jews rescued from the German **concentration camps**. After the war these camps were used to house DPs. Many DPs moved abroad, helped by emigration schemes, to Canada, the United States, Australia, and South America.

The SS *Marine Flasher* arrives in New York, 20 May 1946, carrying over 800 displaced persons admitted to the United States after the war. Many were orphans whose parents were lost in the war or in Nazi concentration camps.

Nations united?

During the war, US President Roosevelt had named the countries opposing Germany and Japan – the United States, USSR, UK, France, and China – as the **United Nations** (UN). In April 1945, a conference was held to establish a new world organization. The United Nations was made official and these countries became full members of the UN.

Dividing up the world

In public, the United States, USSR, UK, France, and China – the **Allied powers** – all agreed to the idea of a **democratic** world where countries would decide on their own futures. In private, they made agreements amongst themselves about who would influence the other countries of Europe. Europe was roughly divided, with countries in the east coming under Soviet **communist** influence and countries in the west coming under Western **capitalist** influence.

The United States, UK, France, and the USSR divided Germany into four zones and each governed their own zone. The capital city of Berlin, which was located in the Soviet zone, was itself divided up into four sectors (see map below).

This map of Europe shows both the Soviet sphere of influence and the Western sphere of influence after the Second World War. Germany was divided into four zones, and its capital Berlin was split into a further four zones.

Capitalist vs communist

The United States feared the system of communism, which the USSR supported. The USSR feared the system of capitalism, which the United States supported. In 1945, the United States was the only country able to put money into the reconstruction of a war-wrecked Europe. The Marshall Plan – named after the US Secretary of State in 1947 – saw billions of dollars pumped into Western Europe. The aim was to speed up economic growth, settle down the political problems, and weaken the appeal of communist parties to western European citizens.

The USSR refused the offer of money from the United States and used its enormous political influence to make sure that countries in Eastern Europe also refused. The Marshall Plan was seen by the USSR as an attempt by the United States to weaken the USSR's power and its communist system. Europe became firmly divided between communist and capitalist powers and Britain's wartime leader, Churchill, spoke of an "iron curtain" dividing the two.

Different points of view

In 1948, the United States supported the introduction of a new currency called the Deutschmark in the western half of Germany. The USSR, who did not want this western currency being used in Berlin, stopped supplies of food and other goods from travelling through eastern Germany to reach the western half of Berlin. The United States responded by flying in supplies by airplane – called the Berlin air lift – until the **blockade** was lifted. From one point of view, the USSR was acting aggressively against west Berlin. From another point of view, the US-backed new currency was an attempt to bring all of Berlin into a capitalist system.

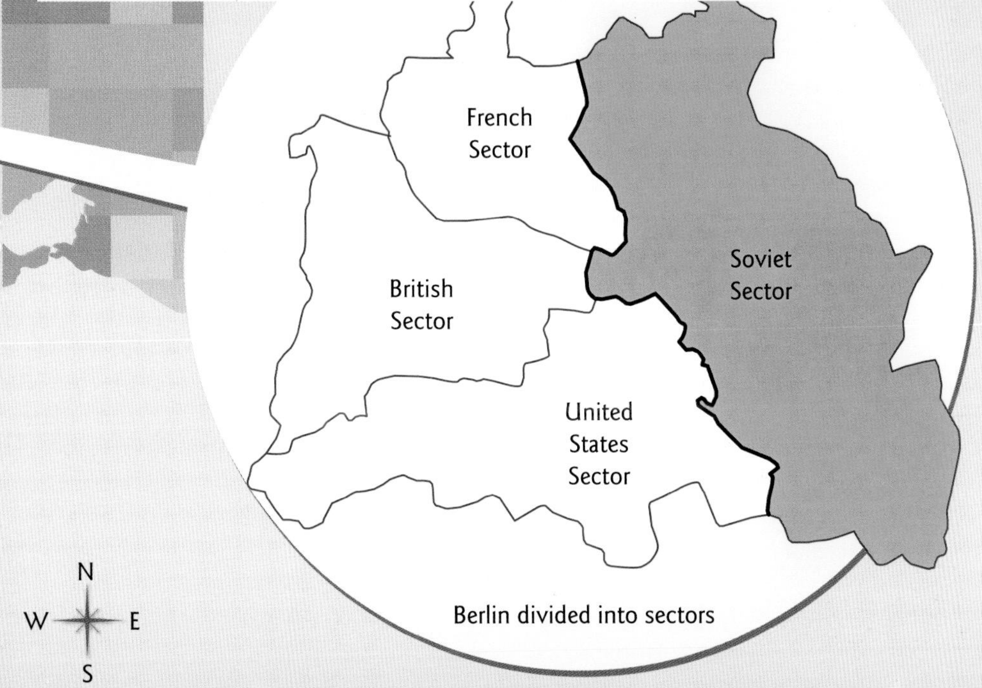

Berlin divided into sectors

NEW TECHNOLOGIES, NEW DESIGNS

The Marshall Plan was very successful and by 1950 Europe was producing 35 per cent more goods than in 1938. Governments introduced **welfare systems** to avoid the poverty of the 1930s. People in the UK began to enjoy new technologies, new designs, and new ways of enjoying leisure time. In 1950, the rationing of milk stopped in the UK and for the first time in nine years people could buy as much milk as they wanted. In 1951, the bacon ration increased from 4 ounces (113 grams) to 5 ounces (142 grams) a week and by 1954 all food rationing came to an end.

Television

When the Second World War ended, television was in its early stages of development. Television programming had begun before the war, but there was only a tiny audience. Television broadcasting to the whole of the UK began in 1946, in France in 1944, and in West Germany in 1952. By 1958, 50 million people, 31 per cent of the population, in the United States owned a television set. By the early 1960s over 90 per cent of US homes received television pictures. Popular US television shows included *The Ed Sullivan Show* (a variety show) and comedies such as *I Love Lucy*.

This US advertisement shows some of the new electrical appliances available during the 1950s, including refrigerators and stoves.

Radio

Radio had been an important part of the lives of millions of people during the war. Wartime radios had been large pieces of wooden furniture. With the invention of **transistors**, radios became small, lightweight objects that could be carried around the house. Sound quality improved enormously and stereo was introduced. In the UK, radio programmes included comedy programmes such as *The Goon Show*, soap operas such as *Mrs Dale's Diary*, and regular news and sports programmes. Radio shows in the United States included sitcoms such as *Life with Luigi*, a story about an **immigrant** family, westerns such as the *Lone Ranger*, music broadcasts, and regular news items.

Consumer boom

By the 1950s, **consumer goods** were flooding on to the market for ordinary people to buy. The German designed, rechargeable Braun electric razor came out in 1954. Vacuum cleaners became cheap and popular, while in the United States Earl Tupper developed a system of plastic storage tubs called Tupperware. These were ideal for storing food in the newly available refrigerators. **Thermoplastics** changed the design of thousands of everyday items because they could be moulded into shape. Microwave cookers were invented, but were too expensive for even wealthy people.

Quiz show scandals

In the 1950s, quiz shows were prime-time television in the United States, where millions watched them. Contestants played for thousands of dollars and if successful one week, returned the next week to risk their winnings once more. In 1958, a scandal broke out when angry former contestants began to admit to the press that they had been given answers to the questions. It turned out that the show's organizers had given answers to the contestants that the audience liked, and let the unpopular ones lose. That year, **US Congress** passed a law making the fixing of a television game show a crime.

Television host Hal March questions a contestant inside the booth during the television quiz show *The $64,000 Question* in 1955.

New fashions

During the Second World War there had been serious shortages of clothes in the countries involved in the war. Silk had been needed for parachutes; factories for making uniforms and weapons; workers for fighting. In the UK, clothes were rationed and were made under the **Utility** label. Utility clothes were aimed at keeping people clothed without wasting resources that were needed for the war. Women's magazines of the time encouraged women to make over their dresses from last year. When the war ended, the shortages continued. Men leaving the armed forces were issued with a demob (demobilization) suit, an inexpensive set of jacket and trousers, to replace their uniforms.

The new look

In the UK and Europe, the hardships of the war continued into the 1950s, but in 1947 the French designer Christian Dior changed women's fashions completely. Instead of practical suits and sensible skirts, Dior's models had narrow waists and long, full skirts using huge amounts of cloth. They were expensive and luxurious. The look was meant to be a change from the clothes of hardship. Dior's designs were only available to the very wealthy, but high street shops began to copy them almost immediately.

A model shows off a luxurious black velvet evening gown from the new collection at Christian Dior, Paris, France, in August 1953.

Make do and mend

Dior's designs were meant for the small number of women with enough money to spend on expensive designer clothes. Ordinary women tried to adapt the clothes they had to the new styles. One woman remembered making a Dior-style skirt out of old **blackout** material. This was the cheap cloth that people in the UK placed over their windows to stop German bombers using house lights to help them identify their targets.

Public reactions

In New York, United States, some women protested against the new look as an unnecessary waste of money and a setback in the fight for women's equality with men. In the UK, politicians discussed the cost to the economy that the manufacture of such expensive clothes would involve. An even bigger fashion revolution came in 1946 when the bikini, named after the island on which the first atom bomb tests were made, became available.

The high street stores

Nylon stockings went on sale in May 1940 in the United States and sold out in four days. Before this stockings had been made of silk, which was very expensive, or wool, which was very coarse. Nylon was cheap, washed well, did not fade, and could be mixed with natural fibres. In the United States department stores such as Macy's and J.C. Penny sold affordable and attractive clothing. In the UK, Marks and Spencer department stores made inexpensive shoes and sensible, easy-to-wash clothes that ordinary women had never been able to afford before. By the late 1950s, these department stores had 50 million customers a week.

Crowds of shoppers swarm the checkouts inside a large UK Marks and Spencer store in November 1955.

Cars and planes

During the war petrol had been rationed in many countries and in the UK, in order to drive anywhere, people had to get local authority permission to use petrol. Cars had been kept in garages until the end of the war. In the United States, rationing ended very soon after the end of the war. There, along with the boom in demand for consumer goods, the car industry exploded. Cars became much more than a way of getting from one place to another. They represented wealth and the freedom of the "open road". Cars grew ever bigger, shinier, and faster with chrome fins and bumpers, big headlights, and a shiny grille on the front. Advertisements suggested that the owners of cars like the 1950 Studebaker, Ford or Mercury were more glamorous and wealthier than people who still used pre-war models.

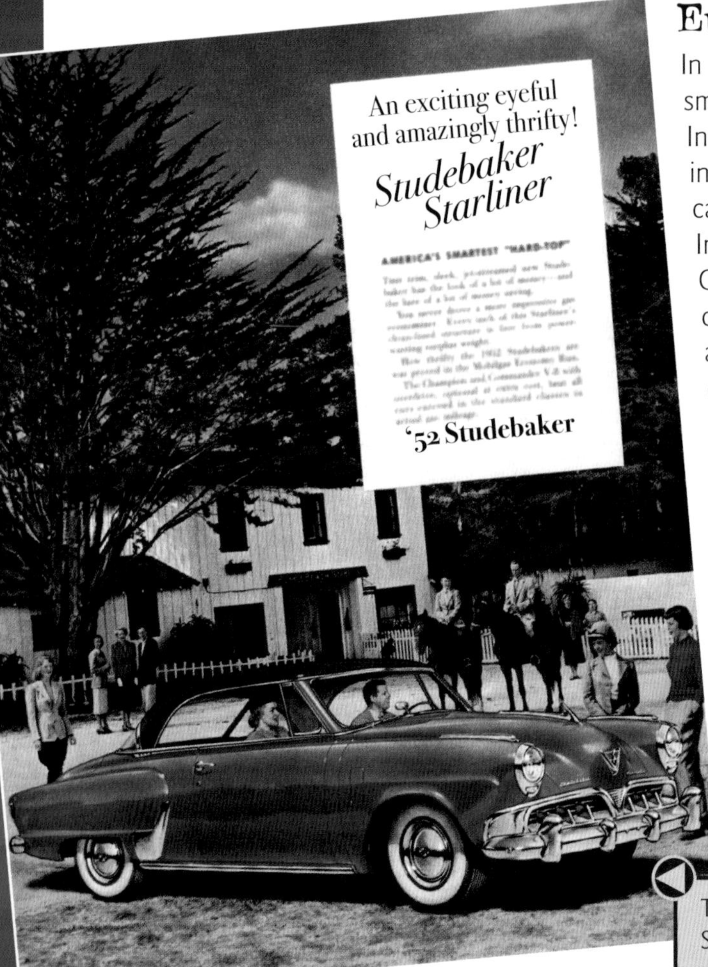

The new, stylish Studebaker Starliner car represented wealth and prosperity in the 1950s in the United States.

European cars

In Europe, cars tended to be smaller and more fuel-efficient. In the UK, the "bubble car" was invented – a tiny three-wheeled car with a front opening hatch. In Germany, the Messerschmitt Cabin Scooter of 1953 was a cross between a motorbike and a car. In Italy, a company developed the Vespa scooter – a motorbike with a tiny petrol engine and a top speed of 50 miles (80 kilometres) per hour. It, and its rival, the Lambretta, became enormously popular in western Europe because they were so stylish.

Commercial jets

The first commercial jet airliner flew in May 1952 when BOAC (British Overseas Airways Corporation) flew a jet from London to Johannesburg in South Africa. In 1957, the Boeing 707 jet aeroplane went into service in the United States. It could carry 180 passengers and signalled the end of the age of great passenger ships.

In the air

Air transport had been in development before the war. European countries had formed national airlines and built small airports near to capital cities. Such developments were abandoned during the war, when all design and manufacture went into fighter planes. After the war the airports returned, and passenger aeroplanes were built with jet engines. Their lighter bodies gave faster speeds for less fuel, while wing flaps and moveable landing gear allowed for better control when landing.

This advertisement shows the popular Lambretta scooter from 1950.

OLD DIVISIONS, NEW COUNTRIES

The Allied powers proclaimed victory in the Second World War as a victory for freedom. After the war, the UK faced demands by its colonies for their freedom. **Nationalism** in the colonies was stronger than ever after the war. These countries refused to be ruled by the British Empire any longer. In the UK, sadness at the loss of the empire found expression in different ways. When an English athlete, Roger Bannister, became the first person to run 1 mile in under 4 minutes in 1954, one newspaper celebrated by proclaiming: "The empire is saved."

India and Pakistan

The government in the UK accepted that it would be wrong to hold on to its empire in India and began to plan for Indian independence – but this was not easy. About two thirds of India's 400 million citizens were Hindu while less than a third were Muslim. The two sides began to fight over who would rule when India gained its independence. One side or the other rejected every plan suggested by the UK. In August 1946, there were riots between Hindus and Muslims in Calcutta and Bengal and 500 people were killed.

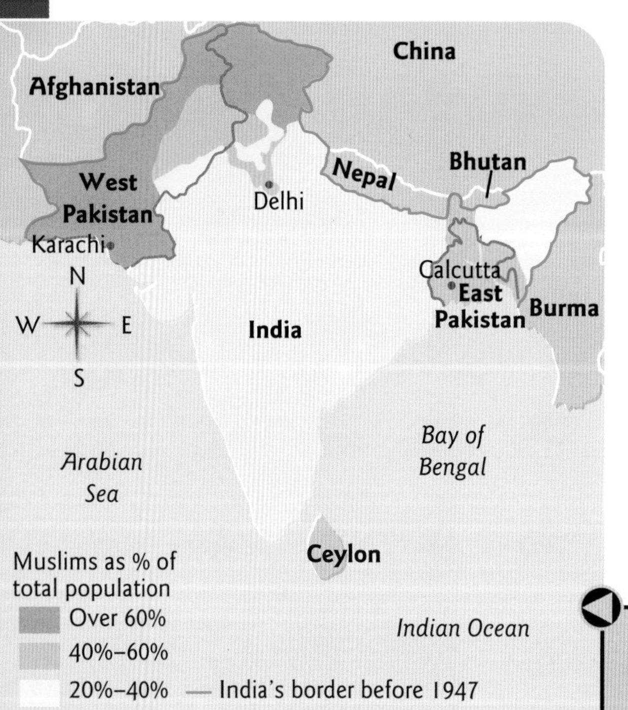

Two states

Faced with increasing violence that it could not stop, the UK government announced in 1947 that it was leaving India. Talks between the UK and representatives of the two groups in India were aimed at finding a way for the two communities to live together. Unfortunately these talks failed. The **Muslim League** demanded an independent Muslim country and the UK agreed to the creation of an entirely new country called Pakistan, made up of the regions where Muslims were the majority.

The map shows the borders of India and Pakistan after an Act of Parliament was passed in 1947 that made them both independent countries.

New borders

In 1947, as soon as the Act of **Parliament** creating the two new countries was passed, millions of Muslims began fleeing from India into Pakistan. Similar numbers of Hindus fled in the opposite direction. Around 10 million people took part in this mass movement. In the chaos about a million people were killed by **extremists** on both sides. Many of those killed were Sikhs, a religious minority in India, who were given no country of their own.

Indian refugees crowd on to trains after the two new countries are created. Muslims flee to Pakistan and Hindus flee to India in one of the largest transfers of population in history.

Gandhi assassinated

Mahatma Gandhi was a very popular leader in India who had always had the support of both Hindus and Muslims. He wanted a single independent country where all Indians could live in peace together. When the fighting broke out, he managed to calm the situation a little. He could do nothing, however, to stop the attacks of one side against the other. Then in January 1948, a Hindu extremist, who was outraged at Gandhi's acceptance of other religions, shot him. Gandhi's **assassination** brought much of the fighting to an end since both sides had greatly respected him. Although the fighting gradually stopped, the tensions between the two countries remained.

Israel and the Middle East

People in the Middle East were also demanding their independence from colonial rule. The UK and France, countries that controlled parts of the region, accepted the demands of nationalist groups as new countries such as Syria and Lebanon gained their independence after the war. In Palestine the situation was more complicated. It was under UK rule, but there were two conflicting groups wanting independence within the country. The majority group of Arabs in Palestine wanted to create an independent Arab state. Palestine, however, also had a community of Jews who felt that they had a claim to a homeland in Palestine. Before Roman times there had been a Jewish state in Palestine, which the Romans had conquered. Many Jews all over the world believed that they had a right to take back that homeland.

Two promises

During the First World War, the UK had wanted help in defeating Turkey in the Middle East. At first, they had promised independence to Arab nationalists in return for their help in fighting the Turks. Later, for the same reason, they also promised to create a national home in Palestine for the Jews. Neither of these promises gave exact details, so both Arabs and Jews could claim the UK had promised them the territory they wanted.

Starting in 1944, UK forces in Palestine came under attack from Jewish groups who were demanding independence. After the war, large groups of Jewish immigrants wanted to settle in Palestine. They were survivors of the Holocaust and they gained international sympathy.

Creation of Israel

The UK handed over the problem of Palestine to the United Nations in 1947. The UN came up with the idea of splitting Palestine between Arabs and Jews. On 14 May 1948, the country of Israel came into existence, whilst the city of Jerusalem remained under international control.

Unanswered questions

The UK Foreign Minister made a statement to **parliament** in 1947, posing questions that faced the UN:

"Shall the claims of the Jews be allowed, that Palestine is to be a Jewish country?
Shall the claims of the Arabs be allowed, that it is to be an Arab country?
Shall it be a Palestinian country where the interests of both communities are as carefully balanced and protected as possible?"

(FROM *MASTERING WORLD HISTORY* BY NORMAN LOWE)

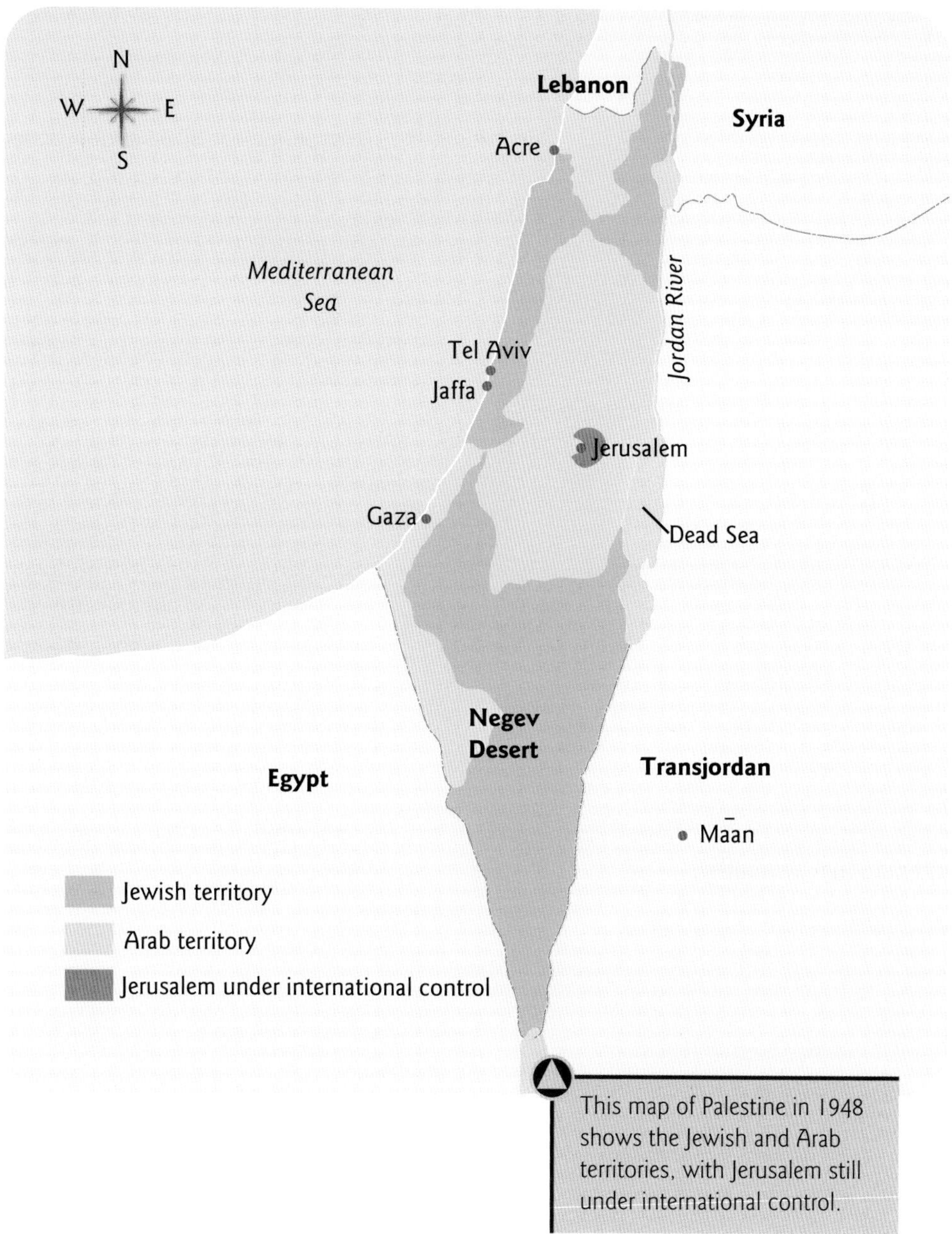

This map of Palestine in 1948 shows the Jewish and Arab territories, with Jerusalem still under international control.

The 1948 war

The day after Israel came into existence, a war broke out as Arab armies from neighbouring countries invaded and attacked Israel. Israel won the war and ended up with about three-quarters of Palestine – far more than the UN had allocated to it. The Palestinian Arabs ended up without a country or a homeland. Some were in the enlarged country of Israel, some in an area taken by Jordan, and hundreds of thousands were expelled by Israel. They became refugees in camps in neighbouring Arab countries, where they still live today.

People's Republic of China

During the Second World War, nationalists in China fought against the Japanese who had invaded their country. The nationalists were divided into a non-communist group and a communist group, which was led by Mao Zedong. Mao's army was more successful in winning the support of the country's **peasants**, but the non-communists felt stronger because of the support of the United States. The result, in 1945, was a **civil war** in China.

Civil war

The United States helped the non-communist forces take over regions of China that had been occupied by the Japanese. Mao's army, however, was better organized and the soldiers were more dedicated and loyal. Many of the leaders of the non-communist forces took money, given by the United States to help them fight their battles, and kept it for themselves. Mao was not **corrupt**, like these other leaders, and his army had a strong belief in what it was fighting for. When the two armies met in battles, the non-communists often surrendered without resistance.

Chairman Mao announces the founding of the People's Republic of China at Tiananmen Square, Peking (Beijing), China, October 1949.

Mao's China

Mao and the communists won the civil war, and the People's **Republic** of China came into existence in October 1949. The defeated non-communist nationalists fled to the Chinese island of Taiwan, refusing to accept Mao's new China.

The invasion of China by Japan had started in 1937 and the twelve years of war had wrecked the economy of China. The tasks facing the communist government of a country of 600 million were enormous, but Mao managed to rebuild the country. Large amounts of land, once owned by wealthy landlords, were distributed to peasants.

Western powers wondered how closely linked China and the USSR might become. They both had communist governments and they were both suspicious of the United States. Mao feared that the United States, which had supported the side that opposed him in the civil war, might try to plan a **counter-revolution** in China. While this brought China and the USSR together, Mao was also very determined to keep the independence of the new Chinese republic.

Tibet

Tibet had been part of the old Chinese empire, but it was not part of China. When the communists took power in 1949, they were determined to regain control of Tibet. In 1950, Chinese forces invaded and Tibetan appeals to the West for help were ignored. In 1959, there was a rebellion against Chinese rule, but it was brutally crushed. The Tibetan leader, the Dalai Lama, went into **exile** in India.

Chinese troops march over the highlands towards the Tibetan frontier after their invasion of Tibet in 1950.

The "loss" of China, and the Soviet atom bomb

In the United States, the success of the communists in China was seen as a major defeat. China was rapidly becoming one of the world's great powers and to have it ruled by communists was seen as a disaster. It came at the same time as the first evidence of the USSR having **atom bombs**. Both events triggered a review of the United States defence policy. If another country had nuclear weapons, the United States had lost its power to threaten them with the atom bomb because now they could do the same. The review recommended increasing spending on non-nuclear weapons from US$13 billion to US$50 billion.

War in South-East Asia

Before the Second World War, Vietnam had been part of the French Empire in Asia. When the war ended, the Vietnamese wanted their independence, but France refused. In 1945, Ho Chi Minh, the Vietnamese leader, declared Vietnam independent. He led a group of nationalists and they attacked the French in what became a nine-year struggle for independence. Because Ho Chi Minh was a communist, France and the United States saw the struggle for independence as a communist threat. In order to stop another communist country emerging in Asia, the United States began to financially support the French side in the war against independence. The new communist country of China supplied Ho Chi Minh's nationalist forces with weapons. The war ended when the French were defeated at Dien Bien Phu in 1954.

French foreign legion soldiers capture and question a Vietnamese nationalist during the Vietnamese fight for independence in 1954.

Vietnam divided

After the French defeat, representatives of all the countries involved attended a peace conference. An agreement was reached, and Vietnam was divided into two halves by a line called the 17th Parallel. Ho Chi Minh's forces controlled the north, and a government friendly to the United States controlled the south. This was to be a temporary arrangement until a general election could create a united country. Ho Chi Minh accepted the agreement because he was so confident about winning a national election.

The government in the south of Vietnam refused to take part in a general election. The United States did not stop this decision, fearing a communist victory. The resulting conflict gradually developed into a civil war and the government in the south came to depend on money from the United States. US citizens, and their leaders themselves, did not realize that supporting the government in the south of Vietnam would lead to the United States' involvement in the Vietnam War from 1954 to 1970.

The map shows Vietnam after the division into North and South Vietnam in 1954; and Malaya, which gained independence from the UK in 1957.

China
Dien Bien Phu
Haiphong
Hanoi
Laos
North Vietnam
17th Parallel
Thailand
Cambodia
South Vietnam
Phnom Penh
Saigon
Malaya
N
W
E
S

War in Malaya

The country of Malaya in South-East Asia was part of the British Empire and here, too, there was a demand for independence after the Second World War. Malaya had a large Chinese population and Chinese communists fought the British, but were defeated in the early 1950s. The British began to re-settle Chinese villagers, suspected of helping the communists, in specially guarded villages. At the same time, independence was promised in the future and the Malay population accepted this, and did not support the rebels. In 1957, Malaya gained independence and later renamed itself Malaysia.

Climbing Mount Everest

While wars were dividing Vietnam and Malaya, two men were climbing the highest mountain in the world, Nepal's Mount Everest, and celebrating **internationalism** when they reached the summit. New Zealander Edmund Hillary and his guide, Tensing Norgay from Nepal, reached the top, 8,848 metres (29,028 feet) above sea level, on 29 May 1953. Hillary described the final ascent:

"It was a beautiful day with a moderate wind. As we got there, my companion threw his arms around me and embraced me. I took photographs of Tensing holding a string of flags – those of the United Nations, Britain, Nepal, and India."

Edmund Hillary and his guide, Norgay, make their historic final ascent to the summit of Mount Everest, 29 May 1953.

THE COLD WAR

The term Cold War came to describe the period after 1945 when the United States and the USSR highly distrusted each other. They were the superpowers of the world and they both tried to influence world affairs in ways that suited their very different ideas about society. Each side thought its economic system was the best. The UK stood firmly on the side of the United States and joined the **North Atlantic Treaty Organization** (NATO), a military **alliance** formed in 1949 with the United States and eleven other countries. Six years later, the USSR formed its own military alliance with other countries, called the **Warsaw Pact**.

The cold war in Asia

Korea, Asia, became the first casualty of United States-USSR rivalry. In 1945, Korea (which had been occupied by the Japanese during the war) was **liberated** by Soviet and US forces. The Soviet and United States' liberators agreed to divide the country between a communist government in the north and a non-communist one in the south. In 1950, North Korea, probably with the backing of the new communist Chinese government, invaded the south in an attempt to **unify** the country. The United States responded by calling on the United Nations to oppose the invasion.

US Airforce B29s drop their cargo of bombs on a strategic target during the Korean War, around 1950.

War in Korea

Troops, mostly from the United States, but from twenty countries in all, were sent to Korea. When these troops pushed into North Korea, China sent in its own forces to push them back. China's confidence in challenging the United States came as a shock to the US generals. They had no idea that China would be so ready to fight them. Some generals including General MacArthur, a Second World War commander, talked of using atom bombs and invading China in order to crush their opposition in Korea. The war turned into a bitter conflict and the US Air Force dropped almost as many bombs on North Korea as had been dropped on Germany in the Second World War.

The North Korean troops treated their prisoners of war very badly, with a third of them dying in the first winter of the war. In one prisoner of war camp there was a rebellion, which was put down with tanks. When a settlement was finally negotiated the last sticking point was the release of prisoners of war. One of the problems was that two thirds of the Chinese prisoners of war refused to return to China, where they would be forced into the Chinese army again.

The wastefulness of war

The Korean War lasted for three years. At the end of it, the division between North and South Korea was exactly the same as it had been at the start. Four million Korean civilians and soldiers lost their lives, and 5 million people were left homeless. About a quarter of a million Chinese soldiers died. United States casualties were 54,000 dead and 100,000 wounded. Of the many other UN forces that took part in the war about 3,000 died, including over 300 Australians.

Korean refugees step through the devastated streets of Inchan, on the west coast of Korea, after a United States attack on the port, 16 September 1950.

Reds under the beds

The **propaganda** of the Cold War affected many aspects of United States life. Communism was seen as a kind of virus. The government began to be concerned that communist spies were in the United States, finding out military secrets and passing them to the USSR. In 1951, engineer Julius Rosenberg and his wife Ethel were found guilty of selling secrets to the Soviets. They were sentenced to death and were executed in New York in 1953, even though there were calls for mercy from all over the world.

Joseph McCarthy

Joseph McCarthy was a **Republican** senator who was not well known in United States politics. But, in 1950, he announced that he had a list of over 200 people working in the **State Department** who were members of the American Communist Party. He never produced a list, or evidence to support his claim, but he aroused fears among many Americans of a secret communist network. McCarthy began a campaign of accusing public figures, such as the playwright Arthur Miller, of being communists. He gained the support of many national newspapers and politicians.

Screenwriter Dalton Trumbo, one of the Hollywood celebrities accused of having links to communism, angrily leaves the witness stand on 28 October 1947.

Un-American activities

In 1952, McCarthy was made head of a committee charged with investigating the loyalty of government employees. All sorts of people, including Walt Disney, were accused of "un-American activities" and this included people who were not communists. Some people protested that McCarthy was in danger of damaging US freedom of speech. Humphrey Bogart and Lauren Bacall, two very famous film stars, took part in a demonstration in Washington against what was happening. Many of those being accused by McCarthy were Hollywood directors and screenwriters. The committee accused government employees, clergymen, lawyers, writers, and even an army general. Thousands of people who had done nothing wrong lost their jobs as a result of McCarthy's accusations: 9,500 civil servants, 600 teachers, and hundreds of actors, writers, and performers lost their jobs. Of those that were accused, 400 went to jail.

A group of Hollywood celebrities, including Lauren Bacall, demonstrate against Senator McCarthy outside Capitol Building, Washington D. C., United States, October 1947.

In June 1953, the hearings led by McCarthy were put on television. When the public watched ordinary-looking people being accused and harassed by the Senator, they began to turn against the hunt for communists. McCarthy was replaced as head of the committee in 1954 and was criticised by the **US Senate** later that same year. The search for communist sympathisers continued, however, and in 1954 a law was passed making the Communist Party illegal.

Reds under the beds

A popular joke term to describe the period of Senator McCarthy's investigation was "reds under the beds." It described the atmosphere of fear that was brought about in the United States in those years when people were worried that communist spies might be bugging their homes, or even hiding under their beds. The term 'reds' came from the fact that the colour red was always the traditional colour of the communist flag.

The Cold War in space

The Cold War resulted in an **arms race** between the United States and the USSR as both sides competed to produce better weapons. As nuclear weapons were now the most powerful weapons possible, a race developed to see who could transport a nuclear bomb to an enemy target in the fastest possible time.

Sputnik

In 1957, the USSR launched *Sputnik*, the first satellite ever to leave Earth and orbit around it. Weighing only 83 kilograms (184 pounds), only 56 centimetres (22 inches) in diameter, and carrying a radio transmitter, *Sputnik* was made to investigate outer space.

United States scientists saw the successful launch of *Sputnik* by the USSR as a terrible defeat for themselves. They felt that Soviet technology had shown itself to be better. A famous scientist, Edward Teller, said on television that the United States had lost "a battle more important and greater than Pearl Harbor."

It took a powerful rocket to launch *Sputnik* and such a rocket, it was feared, could be armed with a nuclear bomb and fired at the United States. A month later *Sputnik II* – weighing half a ton – was launched, this time with a canine cargo of a husky dog called Laika. Laika sadly stopped barking during the flight and presumably died.

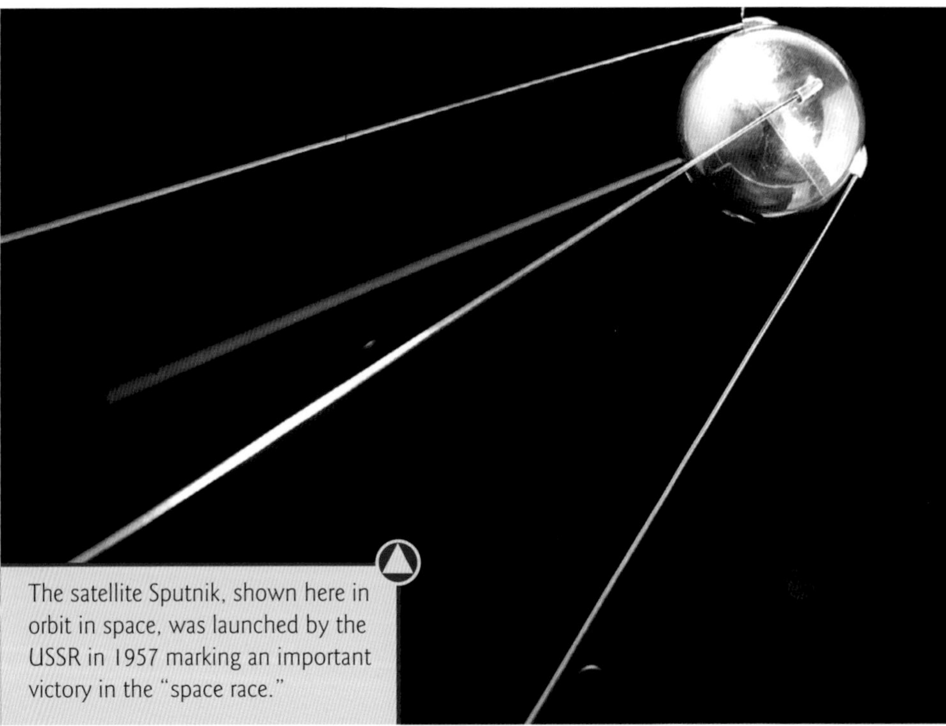

The satellite Sputnik, shown here in orbit in space, was launched by the USSR in 1957 marking an important victory in the "space race."

Vanguard and Explorer

In December of the same year, in a glare of publicity, the United States launched a *Vanguard* satellite. Although at 1.4 kilograms (3 pounds) it was tiny compared to the successful Soviet ones, the attempt failed. The following January, the United States successfully launched *Explorer I* and a series of US satellites followed. The space race had begun and the two countries competed to get the first animals into space and down again alive. Then there was a race to send the first man into space, and to make the first broadcast from space. In the future, President Kennedy would pledge that the United States would be the first to land a man on the Moon.

The "space race"

Huge amounts of money went into the United State's space programme and the National Aeronautics and Space Administration (NASA) was set up. The aim was always to be ahead of the USSR. One air force official, when asked what he expected to find on the Moon, replied "Russians." For other people, though, the space race was about mankind's natural interest in outer space.

The first man in space

On 12 April 1961, a Russian air force major, Yuri Alekseyevich Gagarin, became the first human to travel into space aboard Earth satellite Vostok 1. His journey was a single orbit of Earth, which lasted 1 hour 48 minutes. He travelled at a speed of 17, 000 miles (27,400 kilometres) per hour. Gagarin became world famous as the first man in space. He remained in the USSR air force as a test pilot and was killed in a 1968 crash.

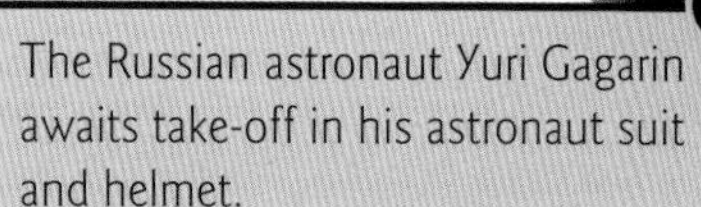

The Russian astronaut Yuri Gagarin awaits take-off in his astronaut suit and helmet.

A CHANGING WORLD

In the UK, the Labour government that had been elected in 1945 came to an end in 1951. A new Conservative government took power, promising better times for the people of the UK. In 1953, the new queen, Elizabeth, was crowned. For working-class people life had improved since the years before the war. The new National Health Service had brought free care to millions of pregnant women. Antibiotics meant that fewer people died of incurable diseases. In 1957, the six European countries France, West Germany, Italy, Belgium, the Netherlands, and Luxembourg formed an economic union, but the UK chose to remain outside.

New leaders

The year 1953 saw a change in leadership for the world's two superpowers, the United States and the USSR. Stalin had been ruling the USSR since 1928 and he had become a cruel **dictator**. He stopped any disagreements with his policies by imprisoning his political opponents, and huge numbers of people died as a result of his dictatorship. People suspected of not supporting the government were sent to labour camps or killed. Stalin died suddenly in 1953 and was eventually replaced by Nikita Khrushchev in 1956.

Good Morning Motherland is a portrait of Joseph Stalin from the Russian school of art.

In the United States there was also a change of leadership. Dwight D. Eisenhower, a Republican, replaced the **Democrat** Harry S. Truman as president in 1953. Eisenhower was a Second World War hero and was seen by many as someone who would manage the country in a more sensible way. An example of this was the way he brought an end to McCarthy's campaign against "reds under the beds."

Eisenhower

Dwight D. Eisenhower was elected the 34th president of the United States in 1952. He had been the commander of the Allied forces during the Second World War and had commanded the invasion of Europe against Nazi Germany in 1944. While he was president he kept the peace with the Soviet Union, while building up US nuclear weapons. He began the United States system of **interstate highways**. This made travel between one US state and another far easier and changed the way that people lived, worked, and travelled. He died in 1969.

Dwight D. Eisenhower greets cheering crowds from the roof of his car during his 1952 presidential election campaign.

The Khrushchev era begins

Khrushchev publicly criticised Stalin's rule, pointing out to the Soviet public the cruelty of his policies and the way people had suffered as a result. Around eight million political prisoners were released from the labour camps.

Khrushchev began a vast house-building programme, encouraged the production of consumer goods, and allowed newspapers more freedom to report the news. He expanded the area of the Soviet Union's farmland by bringing previously **uncultivated** land into use. Khrushchev also put forward the idea that the USSR had to find a peaceful relationship with the United States if nuclear war was to be avoided. It seemed as if a new and less aggressive relationship between the superpowers would now be possible.

Migration

The post-war years saw massive migrations as people, unsettled by the war and the political changes that followed it, found new places to live. The United States took in thousands of people from Europe, Asia, and the West Indies. In 1948, Britain passed a Nationality Act, which granted British citizenship to people of the **Commonwealth** (the countries that had once been ruled by the UK). Workers from Commonwealth countries, where unemployment was high, were encouraged to move to the UK where they were promised jobs.

At first men came alone to the UK from Pakistan, India, and the Caribbean. They were usually offered low paid jobs, doing night shifts in factories, or working long hours as cleaners or kitchen workers. Later, when they were settled, the men brought their families to live with them. Immigrant groups formed small communities within the UK, close to the factories where they worked and usually in the poorest accommodation. Alongside the unskilled labourers came doctors, lawyers, and businessmen who were able to take up these professions in the UK.

The *Empire Windrush* arrives at Tilbury Docks, England, with 482 Jamaican immigrants onboard, June 1948.

The Windrush generation

In the West Indies, people looking for work had preferred to find it in the United States or in Central America, but in 1952 the United States passed a law restricting immigration. The UK took advantage of that and began encouraging families from the West Indies to move to the UK because there was a shortage of workers. The first ship bringing people from the West Indies to the UK as immigrant workers was the *Empire Windrush*, which docked at Tilbury, London, in June 1948. The first generation of people who came to Britain after the war became known as the Windrush generation. In 1953, immigration from the Commonwealth was about 3,000 people a year. By 1957, it was about 47,000 a year.

Discrimination

Immigrants found that life in the UK was not as pleasant as they might have thought. At work they were **discriminated** against and found they were not always welcome when they tried to find somewhere to live. It was not uncommon to find signs hanging in the windows of houses with rooms to rent saying "No Coloureds" or "No blacks or Irish." At the time, this was not illegal.

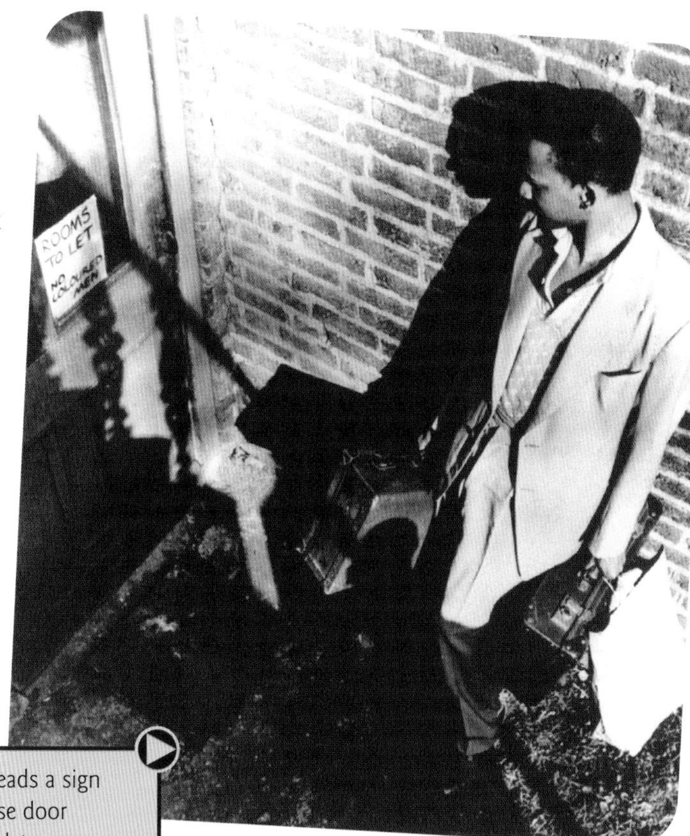

This black immigrant reads a sign on a UK boarding house door which says "Rooms to let – no coloured men," September 1958.

Parliament began to discuss ways of making it illegal to discriminate against people because of their colour or race. A law making racial discrimination illegal was not finally passed until the 1960s. In some London suburbs there were riots against having black people settle in the area. In 1962, Parliament removed the automatic right of Commonwealth citizens to enter the UK freely because they were getting concerned with the threat of large scale immigration.

Multicultural society

While times were quite hard for many immigrants, whatever country they settled in, their arrival added something to the countries that they adopted. The UK, like the United States, had been a place for migrants to settle for hundreds of years, but the wave of immigration of the 1950s eventually brought new ideas in all areas of life from food to music, theatre, politics, medicine, religion, and much more.

Demanding civil rights

In the United States, African Americans began to demand equal civil rights with other US citizens. Many of the 10 per cent of the US population who were black were the descendants of people from Africa who had been kidnapped and brought to the United States as slaves. Even in the 1950s, in some US states, black citizens did not have many of the rights and freedoms of white citizens. Even in states that did not discriminate, some white people thought of black people as their inferiors. In many southern states of the United States, black people could not vote, attend white schools or restaurants, or join **trade unions**. They did the poorest paid work and lived in the poorest conditions. In 1947, President Truman proposed a law to end discrimination, but the **US Congress** rejected the proposal.

As they had done before the war, black people began to challenge each act of discrimination in the courts. In one of these challenges, "Brown vs Board of Education" in 1954, **segregation** in schools was declared illegal. All schools were ordered to accept both white and black students. This caused massive resistance among white people in the southern states who preferred to close their schools down rather than have black students attend.

In 1957, when the schools in Little Rock, Arkansas, United States, were ordered to accept black students, white parents and the governor of the state, Orval Faubus, resisted. Faubus brought in the National Guard to stop black children from entering white schools. President Eisenhower responded by sending in 10,000 troops to enforce the law and protect black children as they attended school.

The US Army is ordered by President Eisenhower to guard black students attending school in Little Rock, Arkansas, United States, October 1957.

Rosa Parks

In Montgomery, Alabama, as in many towns in the southern states of the United States, black people had to give up their seat on a bus if a white person wanted it. In 1955, a black civil rights protestor called Rosa Parks refused to give up her seat to a white man. She was arrested and convicted of disorderly conduct. She appealed against the sentence and eventually the US Supreme Court ruled that segregation on buses was illegal. Her treatment began a year-long-**boycott** by Montgomery's 50,000 black citizens who refused to use the city's buses until they were desegregated. The boycott focussed many people's minds on the issues and made them realize that black people were prepared to take action in order to get equal rights.

The campaign for civil rights

Martin Luther King Jr. became the leader of the civil rights movement, leading **sit-ins** and demonstrations against segregation in the southern states. In many states, black people were afraid to register as voters in case of attacks by racists. The civil rights movement encouraged black people to register, and also supported those that were brave enough to do so.

Rosa Parks sits in the front of a bus in Montgomery, Alabama, after the successful boycott of the city's buses.

Civil rights laws

In 1957, a law was passed that, among other things, set up an investigation into the way black people were being denied the right to vote. This led, in 1960, to a new law that provided official help for black people wanting to register as voters. Progress was being made, but there was still the problem of convincing white people who had been brought up to think of racism as natural, to accept the need for such laws.

Martin Luther King Jr.

Martin Luther King Jr. was a religious leader and one of the leaders of the civil rights movement. He taught people to take part in non-violent protest and persuaded many white people to take up the cause of civil rights.
He toured churches in the United States preaching and fund-raising for the civil rights movement. Later in the 1960s, he led bigger and bigger protests against segregation, many of which were met by police violence. He was imprisoned in 1963 in Birmingham, Alabama. Each peaceful demonstration drew more and more support for black civil rights. In 1964, he received the Nobel Prize for Peace. He was **assassinated** in 1968.

Demanding self-rule

In the years after the Second World War, nationalists in countries that had been ruled by one of the imperial powers – including France, the UK, and the Netherlands – began demanding independence for their countries. The imperial powers dealt with the nationalists in various ways. Sometimes a peaceful agreement was reached. At other times, independence only came as a result of violent struggle.

Independence after violence

In the years after the Second World War, the nationalist majority in the east African state of Kenya, which was a UK colony, wanted independence. The tiny minority of 66,000 white settlers in the country wanted it to remain a British colony. The white settlers hoped to start a conflict with the nationalists in the hope that the UK would get involved and crush the nationalist movement. The whites would then be able to hold on to their power.

The white settlers got their wish in 1952, when a large group called the Mau Mau began a campaign of violence against them and the black people who worked for them. The Mau Mau came mainly from one tribe, the Kikuyu, who had lost much of their best land to white settlers. The UK sent in 100,000 troops and over the next eight years of fighting some 10,000 people, mostly Africans, were killed.

Mau Mau troops line-up at a secret hideout in Meruland, Kenya, December 1963.

Although the Mau Mau were defeated, the UK came to realize that the desire for independence in Kenya was so strong that it would have to be granted. This happened in 1963. Algeria, in North Africa, also had to experience a long and painful war before France finally granted its independence in 1962.

Uprising in Hungary

It was not only the UK and France that were facing demands for independence from the countries that they ruled over. After the Second World War, the USSR had built up its own empire in Eastern Europe. Countries such as Poland, Romania, Bulgaria, and Hungary, were ruled by communist governments that did what the powerful USSR told them to do.

The people of these Eastern European countries did not like their governments being told what to do by the USSR, and in the 1950s they began to make political protests. In 1956, there was a serious challenge to Soviet rule by ordinary citizens in Hungary. A new government came to power and promised to allow other parties to stand for elections.

The USSR was not going to let this happen. Soviet tanks and troops arrived in Hungary's capital, Budapest, and there was fighting in the streets. When the Russian troops had put down the uprising 30,000 people had died. The USSR had made it clear that opposition would not be allowed.

Soviet tanks cross a Budapest street as they move in to crush the Hungarian uprising of October 1956.

New nations

This is a list of some of the nations that gained independence from European powers between 1945 and the early 1960s:

From Britain:
India and Pakistan (1947)
Malaya (1957)
Nigeria (1960)
Jamaica, Trinidad and Tobago (1962)
Northern Rhodesia (later called Zambia) (1964)

From the Netherlands:
East Indies (later called Indonesia) (1949)

From France:
Syria(1946)
Vietnam (1954)
Morocco and Tunisia (1956)
Algeria (1962)

From Italy:
Libya (1951)

From Belgium:
Congo (1961)

Cuba and Castro

At this time Cuba was an independent republic, but US companies owned most of the island's important industries such as sugar, tobacco, textiles, iron, nickel, and copper, and half of the land. What upset poor farmers and factory workers most was Fulgencio Batista, the **corrupt** dictator who seized power in 1952, and who ruled every aspect of their lives.

Social problems

Batista did nothing to improve the lives of ordinary Cubans. Many of them depended on the sugar industry for work, but each year when the harvest was over, unemployment reached 30 per cent. There was no welfare system and most people lived in poverty. Much of the country's wealth was going to United States companies and to a small class of wealthy Cubans.

Fidel Castro

Fidel Castro became a leading nationalist in Cuba. He wanted an end to Batista's corrupt government and a fairer distribution of land to peasants. At this stage he was not a communist and when he began a **guerrilla war** in 1956 against Batista his army was very small.

Batista tried to crush Castro and his guerrilla army but he was not successful. More Cubans supported Castro because of the brutality of the government. Because of this the United States, which had always supported the government, became unwilling to supply any more weapons to Batista's army and cut off its supplies. In January 1959, Batista fled from Cuba and Castro established a new government.

Fidel Castro waves to a cheerful crowd upon his arrival in Havana, Cuba, after Batista fled the country in January 1959.

Who was Che Guevara?

Che Guevara was born in Argentina and became a doctor, but later he joined Castro's guerrilla force in Cuba. He played an important part in forcing Batista to flee and held several important jobs in Cuba as part of the new government. However, he returned to South America in 1966 and joined another guerrilla movement in Bolivia. He was captured and killed there in October 1967.

Images of Che Guevara became very popular in the 1960s, and remain popular, because he died young while fighting for the poor.

A market stall in Cuba sells the popular image of the communist revolutionary Che Guevara on brightly-coloured posters.

Castro and the United States

Relations between Cuba and the United States got much worse. Castro wanted to deal with the island's social problems and his government took control of the country's US-owned oil refineries. This annoyed the United States, which in 1960 placed an **embargo** on all Cuban goods. More industries in Cuba were then taken over by the government and Castro turned to the USSR for help in buying its products.

The United States was convinced that Cuba had become a communist country, and so helped Cuban exiles with plans to invade and overthrow Castro. Cuba began to depend more and more on the USSR for military support and protection. In this way, Cuba's situation became tied up with the Cold War.

EXCITING TIMES

By the late 1950s, Britain was booming. Living conditions for ordinary people were better than they had ever been and education, new technology, and medicines were improving the quality of people's lives. Thousands of ordinary families now owned their own cars and the Sunday drive, when families piled into their car and drove around the countryside, had become a **national pastime**. In 1958, the UK's first motorway, the 8-mile (13-kilometre) long Preston bypass, was opened and in London the first parking meters, with the first parking fines soon being handed out, made their appearance. In the 1959 general election, UK Prime Minister Harold Macmillan used "You've never had it so good" as his campaign slogan.

This advertisement is for hi-fi systems, which brought new technology to ordinary households during the 1950s.

New ideas

Since nuclear energy had first been made use of in 1942, scientists had been developing a way of using it to make electricity. In 1956, the world's first nuclear power station was opened at Calder Hall, Cumbria, UK. The United States quickly followed with a nuclear power station in 1957. By 1959, a more efficient type of nuclear generator was built at Dounray in Scotland. The future seemed bright with this inexpensive and supposedly safe way of producing electricity. In the same year the United States announced that it had developed a tiny atomic generator weighing 2.3 kilograms (5 pounds), which would be used to power equipment in its satellites.

Videos, integrated circuits, and hovercrafts

In other fields of science there were exciting new inventions. Telephones that transmitted pictures, video recorders, the hovercraft, electronic synthesisers, stereo records, and non-stick pans all became a reality. Some of these, such as videos and videophones, took many more years before they became available in the shops, but people were aware of many new technologies in the process of being developed.

New theatre

The experience of the Second World War affected some writers, and in the late 1940s and early 1950s, plays began appearing in the UK and the United States that came to be called the "Theatre of the Absurd." Absurd theatre removes concepts of drama, chronological plot, themes, and recognizable settings. *Waiting for Godot*, by an Irish playwright called Samuel Beckett became world famous as a play about two tramps wandering in a strange landscape, doing nothing except waiting for someone to come and relieve their boredom.

All was not sadness and gloom, however. The 1950s saw large audiences flock to see new musicals such as *The King and I*, *The Sound of Music*, and *West Side Story*.

Strontium 90

During the 1950s, nuclear weapons tests took place around the world. The United States tested its weapons in the Nevada Desert and the Pacific Ocean while the UK's nuclear tests were done in the outback of Australia. In 1958 scientists at Columbia University in the United States discovered that, as a result of the nuclear testing of the previous decade, the amount of radioactive strontium 90 in all the people that they tested had increased by 30 per cent. Strontium 90 collects in human bone and in large enough doses can cause leukaemia (a serious disease) and bone cancer.

A huge mushroom cloud shoots up into the sky above the Pacific Ocean during United States nuclear weapons testing in the 1950s.

The teenager

Before the 1950s, young men and women had worn the same clothes, hairstyles, and shoes as their parents, going from children's clothes to adult clothes as soon as they were old enough. There was little time or money for entertainment, or enjoying being young. The 1950s saw a radical change. As the economies of the West boomed, teenagers had pocket money, part-time jobs after school, and cash to spare.

Unlike their parents and grandparents, teenagers could listen to the music that they liked on the radio, or watch glamorous lifestyle programmes on television. They had enough money to go to the cinema regularly and the entertainment industry realized that here was a valuable new market. Directors began to make films aimed at young people such as *The Wild One*, starring Marlon Brando as a leather-clad biker, or *The Blackboard Jungle*, about a class of rebellious pupils. The young Marilyn Monroe also starred in films of the time such as *Don't Bother to Knock*, in which she played a mentally disturbed babysitter. James Dean was a huge hit with teenagers. Magazines aimed at teenagers sprang up with photos and articles about music stars, fashion, and love stories. Coffee bars became a popular place for teenagers to meet in the UK, while **soda fountains** were where young Americans met. They were places to chat with friends and listen to music on the jukebox.

Rocking and rolling

The new music and new money created teenage fashions. After 1955, teenagers had their own dances and, to show off on the dance floors, young people began to want their own styles of clothes. Girls began to wear tight sweaters, full knee-length skirts with tight waists over layers of nylon petticoats, flat shoes, and white socks instead of stockings. As the girls twisted and turned on the dance floor the skirts flared out. Boys wore checked shirts, leather jackets, denim jeans, and T-shirts.

A teenage girl selects a song from the jukebox in The Little Soda Fountain in Manila, Philippines, around 1956.

James Dean

The clothes that teenagers wore and the music they listened to shocked and outraged the older generation. A few figures seemed to sum up this sense of rebellion. One of these was James Dean, a young actor whose screen roles, especially in *Rebel Without a Cause*, came to represent the problems of being young. He was nominated for two Oscars, but died in a car crash at the age of 24. His tragic death at such a young age made him an **idol**.

Rebel Without a Cause, the popular teenage movie starring James Dean and Natalie Wood, was filmed in 1955.

Rock and roll

Before the Second World War, music played and listened to by black people was called "race music," and in the 1920s and 1930s it had a major impact on the music scene. By the 1950s, jazz had become more of a **cult genre**, popular with a group of intellectual young people known as "beatniks". After the war, with the easier availability of record players and the desire of young people to choose their own music, "race music" included another style called R & B (rhythm and blues) and it began to be played on radio stations that young white people listened to. Record companies began to produce versions of R & B tunes sung and played by white artists, and so rock and roll was born.

The first rock and roll song is widely believed to be "That's All Right Mama" by Elvis Presley, released in 1954. However, this is still debated – some think rock and roll started as early as 1951 with "Rocket 88" by Jackie Bentson.This was followed by a hit called "Shake Rattle and Roll" by Bill Haley and the Comets. In 1955, they had a worldwide hit with "Rock Around the Clock." Chuck Berry in the United States and Lonnie Donegan in the UK had hits with rock and roll music. Donegan's band featured someone playing a washboard (a ribbed board used to scrub washing clean) and was called skiffle music.

American rock and roll singer Elvis Presley performs "Hillbilly Heartbreak" on stage in Hollywood, California, United States, 22 June 1956.

Another rocker was Little Richard whose performance on stage was as exciting as his music. All over Europe and the United States, in bedrooms and garages, young people began copying the sound of these new musicians. The music was played on jukeboxes in coffee bars and soda fountains. Teenagers listened to the music and dreamt of playing it themselves one day. In Liverpool, four boys grew up to become The Beatles and went on to become one of the most successful bands ever.

The rock and roll sensation of the 1950s was Elvis Presley. His first hit in the United States, in 1956 was "Heartbreak Hotel." His singing style was a mixture of the music of southern blacks and the new teenage rebelliousness. As he sang he danced in a way that no white performer had ever done before. He was good looking and like the boy that no parent wanted their daughter to go out with – girls loved it. He wore his hair long and slicked back, with long sideburns; this was the style of street gangs. In the UK, pop singers with names like Billy Fury, Adam Faith, and Cliff Richard copied Elvis' style, hoping to become the English Elvis. Elvis had become the world's first music superstar, just as Charlie Chaplin, Judy Garland, and Humphrey Bogart had become superstars in film and theatre.

Chuck Berry was one of the most popular US rock and roll stars of the 1950s.

Elvis cuts his hair

By 1958, Elvis was a rock star and a film star, but his career came to a temporary end when he was **conscripted** into the US Army in 1958. His manager, Colonel Parker, made the event into a publicity stunt and Elvis was filmed having his long hair cut into an army crew cut. When he emerged two years later Elvis was clean cut and his songs were smoother. He concentrated on his film career, making an album for each film, filled with ballads. He became the idol of the whole family.

DANGEROUS TIMES

In 1953, with the war in Korea over, the elderly British Prime Minister, Winston Churchill, called for a friendly conference of the world powers. For a while it seemed as if relations might improve between the United States and the USSR and there was a mood of optimism. In 1955, UK, French, Soviet, and United States' representatives met in Geneva and there was talk of "peaceful co-existence."

By the early 1960s, however, this mood began to disappear. The UK's Conservative government believed in the need for nuclear weapons as a **deterrent** to the threat of invasion from the USSR, which they saw as a serious threat. In 1961, the Labour Party also decided to support the case for nuclear weapons.

Spy plane shot down

A meeting between the Soviet, United States, UK, and French leaders was due to take place in Paris in May 1960. The Soviet leader, Khrushchev, spoke of an "optimistic" mood affecting the chances of world peace. Suddenly, just before the conference was to begin, Khrushchev announced that a US spy plane had been shot down over Soviet territory. The pilot, Gary Powers, had parachuted out and was arrested after landing safely.

US Air Force pilot Gary Powers prepares to board a jet. His spy plane was shot down over the USSR in May 1960.

Bad feelings

The shooting down of the spy plane meant that Cold War bad feelings began to rise to the surface once more. Khrushchev arrived at the conference in Paris demanding an apology from the United States, for sending spy planes over the USSR. President Eisenhower refused to do so and the Soviet leader stormed out of the conference. The Cold War was up and running once again.

Ban the bomb

Opposition to the UK's decision to build nuclear weapons was growing. In April 1961, a public demonstration calling for nuclear **disarmament** took place in the UK, marching from the nuclear weapons base at Aldermaston, Berkshire to London. More people took part than ever before. Some of the protestors called for non-violent **direct action** and in May 1961 around eight hundred people were arrested at a sit-down protest in London. People were also arrested in Scotland where US nuclear submarines were based. After another protest in London in September 1961 over 30 people were sent to prison, but the protests continued and over 1,300 people were arrested in London's Trafalgar Square for sitting down and refusing to move.

Nuclear protesters carry out a sit-down protest outside Whitehall, London, UK on 18 February 1961.

What happened to Gary Powers?

Gary Powers, the pilot of the spy plane, was put on trial in Moscow in August 1960. He pleaded guilty to spying, admitting that he had been illegally flying over the USSR. In his crashed plane, pictures of Soviet airfields were found. Powers was sentenced to ten years in prison, but was released two years later when he was exchanged for a Soviet spy caught by the United States.

The Berlin Wall

One city, two systems

Even though Berlin was a city in East Germany, the half of the country that was under Soviet control, the city itself was divided into two halves. One half was being run by the communist government of East Germany, and the other was run by the pro-United States West German government. Germans could move freely between the two parts of the city: the western part, under United States, French, and UK influence, and the eastern part, under Soviet influence.

This was causing a problem for East Germany because, since 1945, around 2 million of its citizens had chosen to go and live in the wealthier West Germany. Although the border between East and West Germany had been closed since 1952, they could travel to east Berlin and freely cross into the western part of the city. Once there, the government helped them reach West Germany using the protected air route that connected west Berlin with West Germany.

Brain drain

Over the first six months of 1961, the number of East Germans leaving through Berlin was rapidly increasing. Nearly 20,000 had left in March alone and the country's economy was being affected. Many of those leaving were professionals and skilled workers, leaving behind jobs that could not easily and quickly be filled.

East German soldiers build the Berlin Wall even higher to separate East and West Berlin, 1 October 1961.

Building the Wall

On 12 August 1961, Berliners started to hear news about a barrier of barbed wire being built across their city by the East German authorities. In the days that followed, the barbed wire was replaced by concrete blocks and a solid wall divided the two parts of the city. Some people's homes stood inside East Berlin, but their front doors opened into West Berlin. The army blocked up the doors and people escaped through their windows. In June 1962, a man trying to cross the Wall was shot and killed by an East German guard. Another 191 people would die trying to escape from East Berlin before the Wall finally came down in 1989.

The Berlin Wall became a symbol of the world that the post-war decade had made. The world had become divided, like Berlin, into two halves, opposed to each other and with the capability of wiping each other out. It would be almost 30 years before the Wall was no longer needed. The decade had seen huge changes in technology and for Westerners at least there was a better quality of life. The term "teenager" had been born and so had rock and roll. Television and films had become everyday forms of entertainment. Cars got bigger and radios got smaller. It was an exciting time to be alive.

Only a white line

Before the Berlin Wall was built, the boundary between the two halves of the city was in places only a white line painted on a road. Each of the two halves of the city had its own police force, its own army, and its own currency. At the same time, though, buses and trains followed their traditional routes across the city. So, too, did the city's telephone lines. When the Wall was built, people would stand on ladders to wave to their relatives who lived on the other side.

East German police carry 18-year-old Peter Fechter's lifeless body. He was shot by communists whilst trying to escape to the West on 17 September 1962.

TIMELINE

1940
Nylon stockings go on sale in the United States

1945
The United Nations is formed
Korea is liberated and divided into two states

1946
Riots in India

1947
The Marshall Plan to help European countries rebuild their economies is established
Dior launches the new look
Civil war in China
Exodus in India
Winston Churchill first coins the expression "The Iron Curtain"

1948
Blockade of west Berlin begins
Country of Israel is established

1949
USSR develops nuclear weapons
The United States passes a law restricting entry to communists
The People's Republic of China is established

1950
North Korea invades South Korea
China invades Tibet
The new Studebaker is put on sale

1951
The Rosenbergs are sentenced to death in the United States
McCarthy begins search for communists

1952
Peace settlement in Korea
Coronation of the Queen in the UK

1953
McCarthy hearings televised
Edmund Hillary climbs Mount Everest
Death of Stalin

1954
Rationing ends in the UK
Roger Bannister breaks the 4 minute mile
French defeated at Dien Bien Phu

1955
Rosa Parks case in the United States

1956
Hungarian uprising
World's first nuclear power station is opened

1957

Boeing 707 jet airliner comes into service
Malaya gains its independence
Sputnik I is launched
Civil rights dispute in Little Rock, Arkansas leads to civil rights law

1958

Quiz-show scandals in the United States
First motorways in the UK

1959

Batista flees Cuba
Rebellion in Tibet crushed

1960

United States has 50 million television sets
UK revokes right of entry to Commonwealth citizens

1961

First man in space

1962

Algeria gains its independence

1963

Kenya gains its independence

FURTHER INFORMATION

Books

Armies of the Past: Going to War in World War II, Moira Butterfield (Franklin Watts, 2001)
Hitler's Rise to Power and the Holocaust, Linda Jacobs Altman (Enslow, 2003)
Leading Lives: Ho Chi Minh, Philip Steele (Heinemann Library, 2003)
Leading Lives: Martin Luther King, David Downing (Heinemann Library, 2002)
Teen Witnesses to the Holocaust: In the Camps: Teens Who Survived the Nazi Concentration Camps, Toby Axelrod (Rosen, 1999)
The Cuban Missile Crisis in American History, Paul Brubaker (Enslow, 2001)
The History of Rock and Roll, David Shirley (Franklin Watts, 1999)
The Story of the Holocaust, Clive A. Lawton (Franklin Watts, 2000)
20th Century Design: The 40s & 50s War and Post War Years, Helen Jones (Heinemann Library, 2000)
20th Century Fashion: The 40s & 50s: Utility to New Look, Helen Reynolds (Heinemann Library, 1999)
20th Century Media: The 1940s & 50s: The Power of Propaganda, Steve Parker (Heinemann Library, 2003)
20th Century Music: The 40s & 50s From War to Peace, Jackie Gaff (Heinemann Library, 2002)

Websites

http://en.wikipedia.org/wiki/1900s
Wikipedia encyclopedia with sections on the 1940s and the 1950s.

www.geocities.com/historygateway/1900.html
Weblinks to interesting sites relevant to the history of women in Britain.

http://kclibrary.nhmccd.edu/decades.html
A history site dedicated to United States cultural history on a decade-by-decade basis.

http://charter.uchicago.edu/AAH/19001940.htm
African-American history.

Disclaimer

All the internet addresses (URLs) given in this book were valid at the time of going to press. However, due to the dynamic nature of the Internet, some addresses may have changed, or sites may have ceased to exist since publication. While the author and publishers regret any inconvenience this may cause readers, no responsibility for any such changes can be accepted by either the author or the publishers.

the mid 1940s to the early 1960s

Books and literature	• A new group of anti-establishment authors, called The Beat generation (or Beatniks), include the author Jack Kerouac and poet Allen Ginsberg • Science fiction becomes more popular with the actual possibility of space travel • Anne Frank's moving diary is published in 1952
Education	• Elizabeth Eckford is the first black teenager to enter the all-white Little Rock Central High School, Arkansas, United States in 1957
Fads and fashions	• Silly Putty is sold worldwide by the 1960s • The Hula-Hoop is introduced in 1958 and sells 24 million in just 2 months
Historic events	• Russia puts the first woman into space in 1963. Lieutenant Valentina Tereshkova circled the earth in a *Vostok* space ship. • US Presidents are limited to a maximum term of eight years in office from 1951
Music, film, and theatre	• Drive-in movies become popular in the United States
People	• US rock and roller Buddy Holly dies in an airplane crash in 1959 • Marilyn Monroe is found dead in her bed in 1962

GLOSSARY

alliance military or social agreement between two or more countries
Allied powers countries at war against Germany and Japan in the Second World War
arms race competition between countries to have more powerful weapons
assassinate to deliberately target and kill someone
atom bomb weapon of mass destruction releasing an atom's energy
Berlin Wall long barrier built to divide East and West Berlin
bankrupt unable to pay one's debts
blackout extinguishing all forms of light to prevent being detected by an enemy
blockade methods used to prevent something happening
boycott refuse to have anything to do with a person or a group as a form of protest
capitalist someone who believes in an economy based on private ownership and profits
civil war war taking place within a country, not against a foreign country
Cold War period of hostility between the United States and the USSR that existed from 1945 until the late 1980s
colony country ruled over by another country as part of an empire
Commonwealth group of countries once part of the British Empire
communist someone who believes in government ownership and spreading wealth
concentration camp prison camp where people are forced to live
conscripted called up into the army
consumer goods things that ordinary people need to buy
corrupt not honest
counter-revolution second revolution after the first one has failed
cult genre someone or something that is highly regarded by a minority of enthusiastic followers
Democrat member of the Democrats, a political party in the United States
democratic free elections and the free choice of political representatives
deported expelled from a country or region
detention camps places where people are kept, against their will, until a decision has been made about their future
deterrent something that puts you off doing something
dictator single ruler with all the power
direct action taking action that will be noticed in order to support a cause
disarmament removal of weapons
discriminate to make a choice on the basis of, for example, race or religion
displaced person the name given to the thousands of people who ended up in the wrong country at the end of the Second World War
economy matters to do with money
embargo ban on trade of something with another country
empire control of other countries by a dominant power
ethnic minority smaller group with their own identity
exile expelled from one's own country, usually for political reasons
extremist unwilling to easily reach agreement in a dispute

guerrilla war form of fighting against larger and more powerful forces which avoids an open battle

gulag harsh labour camp

Holocaust murder of European Jews and other ethnic groups

idol someone who is greatly admired

internationalism policy of co-operation between countries

interstate highway main road connecting two US states

liberate set free

Muslim League Indian political organization created in 1906 to protect the rights of Muslims in India

national pastime activity or hobby that most people in a country enjoy

nationalism desire for self-government in a country ruled over by another country

North Atlantic Treaty Organization (NATO) defence organization whose members were Canada, Denmark, France, Iceland, Italy, Luxembourg, the Netherlands, Norway, Portugal, UK, and the United States. Greece and Turkey were admitted in 1952 and West Germany in 1955.

parliament place where politicians make decisions and pass laws

peasant poor person who works on the land

propaganda information that presents only one point of view

rationed equal sharing out of something in short supply

refugee person who has no home

republic form of government without a king or queen

Republican member of the Republican political party in the United States

segregation treating people differently, according to their race

sit-in form of political protest where large numbers of protestors refuse to leave a building, making it unusable

soda fountains name for the soft drinks bars in the United States

Soviet having to do with the USSR

State Department government department in the United States dealing with domestic matters

thermoplastic material that goes soft when it is heated

total war war in which nearly every country in the world is involved

trade union organization formed by workers to protect their interests

transistor small semi-conductor which is used as a circuit in electrical equipment

uncultivated farmland that has been lying idle and unused

unify organize into a single political unit

United Nations international organization of countries. Its role is to achieve international co-operation in solving economic, social, cultural, or humanitarian problems.

US Congress the law-making body of the United States

US Senate part of the law making body of the United States

USSR Union of Soviet Socialist Republics

Utility label put on goods by the UK government to approve them as useful to the war effort

Warsaw Pact military alliance of seven European Communist nations, signed in 1955, and dominated by the USSR

welfare system government-run scheme to help the poorer members of a country

INDEX